SAFE

Alexis Gregory

SAFE

OBERON BOOKS
LONDON

WWW.OBERONBOOKS.COM

First published in 2017 by Oberon Books Ltd
521 Caledonian Road, London N7 9RH
Tel: +44 (0) 20 7607 3637 / Fax: +44 (0) 20 7607 3629
e-mail: info@oberonbooks.com
www.oberonbooks.com

PB ISBN: 9781786823380
E ISBN: 9781786823397

Cover design by Yanny Tokyo

Printed and bound by Marston Book Services, Didcot, UK.
eBook conversion by CPI Group (UK) Ltd, Croydon, CR0 4YY.

A 2015 survey found that 25% of homeless and at risk young people in the UK identify as LGBT.

The Albert Kennedy Trust is a charity that helps and supports homeless and at risk LGBT youth.

This verbatim piece has been created out of interviews with AKT service users.

Each character is based on one individual; not an amalgamation of various interviewees.

All character names have been changed.

Foreword

Tim Sigsworth MBE, Chief Executive of The Albert Kennedy Trust, came to see my debut play, *Slap*, at Theatre Royal Stratford East. We met for the first time in the bar, afterwards. He suggested that due to *Slap*'s gay and trans themes, the young people he came into contact with via the AKT may like the play. A couple of months later, at an awards ceremony, I was sat next to Susannah Clay and Tony Butchart-Kelly, then Communications Officer at the AKT. Tony suggested that I, as an actor as well as a playwright, may be able to coach some of the charity's young ambassadors: ex-AKT service users, now representing the charity and the amazing, vital work they do, in terms of their public speaking and media appearances.

A few weeks later, Tim, Tony and myself sat around a table in a coffee shop in Hoxton, trying to work out exactly how I could get involved with the AKT. By the end of the meeting, I had told them that I was going to create a verbatim play, not my usual style of writing, created entirely out of my interviews with the AKT's LGBT youth, and that the play was going to be called *Safe* and so, that was that and there wasn't any turning back.

Tony introduced me to three wonderful young people. We all met over one weekend at the charity's office, so that I could interview them, shaping the play in my head as I did so. We talked a lot that weekend. And then we talked some more!

At the start of the process, I was a stranger to the young people. By the end of it, they had shared their innermost moments with me; their pain, their joy, their rock-bottom moments and the moments when they fought back and survived. I think it was an extraordinary weekend for us all. I met the fourth interviewee, who eventually was renamed as 'Alicia' in the script, over Skype a few weeks later, and shared a similar experience with her.

Director Robert Chevara, one of my ongoing collaborators, came on board without seeing the as-then-unfinished script. He just knew that he wanted to help me realise my vision for the piece and highlight these stories from our community's most vulnerable and unheard members. I was asked by Duncan Day, of the Pride in London Arts Festival, to present a first performance of *Safe* at the Soho Theatre. It sold out. Some of the young people whose stories were portrayed on stage came to see it. That was the first time I met the 'real' Alicia. Some of the young people couldn't come. They were still dealing with their own and ongoing daily problems.

London Theatre Workshop generously supported a run for the piece and we sold out again, as audiences came together to witness these extraordinary stories unfold as performed by our stunning, committed casts. The young people who shared their stories with me – to process their pain, celebrate their survival and help other LGBT youth – have since become friends of mine. As their stories do not have nice, tidy, resolute endings, I've continued to witness some of their ongoing struggles. I've also since witnessed their successes. *Safe* is dedicated to them, in their journey towards security, acceptance, freedom and equality.

Alexis Gregory,
August 2017

Alexis Gregory would like to thank:

Tim Sigsworth MBE, Susannah Clay
and all at the Albert Kennedy Trust

Arts Council England

Attitude Magazine

Rikki Beadle Blair MBE and John Gordon at Team Angelica

Paul Burston

Tony Butchart-Kelly

Skye Crawford, Ray Rackham
and all at London Theatre Workshop

Steven Crocker

Duncan Day

Cliff Joannou

Norwich Theatre Royal

Pride In London

Soho Theatre

Characters

JACK

A young trans man who identifies as gay.
Boyish, full of quiet strength and determination.

The actor playing Jack is also referred to as
ACTOR 1 in the script.

TAMI

A young trans woman. Smart, streetwise,
tough yet vulnerable, glamorous.

The actor playing Tami is also referred to as
ACTOR 2 in the script.

SAMUEL

A young, black, gay man, Nigerian born.
Intelligent, charming, funny, full of energy.

The actor playing Samuel is also referred to as
ACTOR 3 in the script.

ALICIA

A young gay female. Eloquent, mature,
on her journey to recovery.

The actor playing Alicia is also referred to as
ACTOR 4 in the script.

THE SINGER

Someone with a unique style of singing;
edgy, real and raw.

NOTES ON STAGING

The piece is to be played on a bare stage, unfurnished apart from four chairs. No props.

All actors double up, as indicated, as characters in each other's stories.

Characters talk to the audience and to each other.

As the piece moves forward, moments can be 'set' in specific locations; bedrooms, family homes, on public transport, etc. or in a more neutral 'no man's land' that the characters can inhabit too. Stage directions and actions don't have to be limited by any means to those in the script.

An '–' indicates that the line of dialogue is continued by the next actor or follows on immediately from the last.

Safe was first performed at the Soho Theatre on 26 June 2015. Cast and creatives were as follows:

THE SINGER	Kamali Franklin
JACK	Nelsy Casallas
TAMI	Jennifer Daley
SAMUEL	Urban Wolf
ALICIA	Emma White
Director	Robert Chevara
For Pride in London	Duncan Day
For Soho Theatre	Peter Flynn and Catherine McKinney

Safe was then performed at London Theatre Workshop from 17 – 22 October 2016. Cast and creatives were as follows:

THE SINGER	Rudi Douglas and Tori Allen-Martin
JACK	Riley Carter Millington
TAMI	Kit Redstone
SAMUEL	Michael Fatogun
ALICIA	Laura Jayne Ayres
Director	Robert Chevara
Lighting Design	Nao Nagai
Make-up Design	Victoria Winfield

Safe transferred to Norwich Theatre Royal on 28 September and 29 September 2017. Cast and creatives included:

Director	Alexis Gregory

As the audience enter the space, music is playing; loud, really loud.

'Blind' by Hercules and Love Affair.

'Faggot' by Meshell Ndegeocello.

'After the Love' by Boy George.

'Fistful of Love' by Antony and the Johnsons.

THE SINGER steps into the empty space and performs an acoustic version of 'Small Town Boy' by Bronksi Beat.

Just ahead of the song finishing, JACK, TAMI, SAMUEL and ALICIA enter and each take a seat, for now. They are in the interview room to be interviewed for 'Safe'. They face out and introduce themselves to the audience and the now non-existent interviewer.

JACK	Jack.
TAMI	Tami.
SAMUEL	Samuel.
ALICIA	Alicia.
JACK	At what point do you want me to start talking? I'm quite excited. Everybody likes answering questions about themselves!
SAMUEL	I've shared my story a lot. It isn't a decision I've made. I'm an opportunist. I take whatever comes my way.
ALICIA	There was a time when I couldn't even talk to myself about my story.
JACK	I'm going to be really honest though.
ALICIA	Now I'm like 'go on, liberate yourself'.
SAMUEL	Is that what you're going to record us on? An iPhone? It's just that I thought your equipment would be a bit more…professional.

TAMI I'd like to be heard and understood. What do you want to know? I'll tell you everything.

JACK Obviously, I was born female. It was early on that I noticed that that wasn't right. I was probably about four and I was completely convinced that there had been a mistake and I was going to grow the appropriate body parts and grow up to become a boy and things would change and everything would become right. And then that didn't happen.

SAMUEL I was brought up in Nigeria. I came here when I was eighteen. In school I knew I was a bit different, I was attracted to guys. I didn't know the 'gay' word or what homosexual meant. I thought I was the only person attracted to guys.

TAMI I identified as a gay boy, but more as a feminine gay boy.

ALICIA I was five when I kissed my best friend at school. The older girls saw and from that age I was called names based on that. Words like –

ACTOR 2 *(Jumping up out of seat.)* 'Lesbian!'

ALICIA – and –

ACTOR 3 *(Jumping up out of seat.)* 'Dyke!'

ALICIA – were used as insults. I didn't even know those words.

JACK And then over time I realised this was something I shouldn't be saying as I sort of said about it and nobody took any notice or it wasn't received very well.

SAMUEL I actually have a problem with the word 'homosexual'. From where I'm from it's a negative word.

When my parents use it it's to demean someone, to bring them down so I prefer the word 'gay'.

TAMI   There were times when I went to school wearing make-up. I used to steal my mum's. I never wore make-up at home. I used to take mascara and eyeliner and all the kids would laugh at me but it didn't bother me. I wanted to be the attention seeker but then that got me into trouble too.

SAMUEL   In primary school there was a girl I liked but I liked her brother more!

ALICIA   I was ten or eleven and I said to my mum, 'the girls at school are calling me a lesbian, does that mean I am?' and my mum said –

ACTOR 2   'Of course you're not. Don't be ridiculous. You know you like boys.'

JACK   I'd had a lot of depression and drug use in my teenage years because of stress to do with the way my body was changing. I really couldn't handle it. I ended up doing the tomboy thing because I thought it was the only thing I could do and then I got to about seventeen or eighteen and I thought, well what am I? I remember the conversation I had with myself and it was really separate, picking it apart, trying to work out what the fuck I was and I thought well, I'm a tomboy who's grown up and I thought what's that? And I thought *(joyous, elated realisation)* 'it's a dyke!' and then I thought *(sudden doubt)* 'Am I a dyke?'

ALICIA   I sort of went from each sexuality trying to find the right one. It started when I was fifteen or fourteen and I thought I was bisexual and then at eighteen I came out as gay.

TAMI   I came out as gay when I was eleven years old. I had my first sexual encounter at twelve *(TAMI gets up off her chair and provocatively prowls the stage.)* at school with another pupil three or four years older than me. It was confusing but exciting. I'd had a slice of the cake or the forbidden fruit that had fallen from the tree. I picked it up and tasted it.

ALICIA   When I look back now to myself at a young age I wasn't straight at all, it was pretty blatant but I just pushed it down.

SAMUEL   My parents had an idea of black kids coming here from Nigeria and getting corrupted, westernised and becoming something else. They didn't want us to become 'Bad Western Kids'. We weren't allowed to have friends as they thought they would corrupt us and tell us things we shouldn't be hearing and make us do things we shouldn't be doing. We had curfews. Once we got into trouble for going out without telling them and we got back late about eight thirty pm and we all had to sleep outside in the cold. We weren't allowed back in.

TAMI   It took me a year to tell my mother. Her reaction wasn't loving. We went to my mum's friend's house and I was playing upstairs with my mum's friend's kids and I told them that I was gay and they came downstairs and told my mother. I was thirteen and she called my name very loudly, my male name which was –

ACTOR 4 suddenly comes forward, at a family friend's house now and at the bottom of the stairs, shouting ups them, furious and in her own pain.

ACTOR 4   'DYLAN!'

TAMI   And I went down and she said to me –

ACTOR 4   'Are you gay?'

TAMI   And I said 'yeah I'm gay' and she punched me
               in the face.

*ACTOR 4 strikes out and even though TAMI is on another part of the
stage, her head violently flips back as she receives the blow. After a second,
she recovers, composes herself, still breathless and winded though.*

TAMI   I cried my eyes out, left the house, ran away and
               didn't come back until a week later.

TAMI scurries away.

ALICIA   My dad who is very homophobic and very small
               minded on every topic and would probably vote
               UKIP, if he was inclined to vote, started saying
               more and more when I was a teenager that if I
               ever got pregnant, if I ever had a boyfriend from
               a certain background or if I was ever a lesbian
               or bisexual he would put my head through the
               wall.

SAMUEL   We all got beaten up at different times. Once
               my dad sent my sister to get groceries and she
               came back late. She said there was traffic and he
               said that she'd gone somewhere else and so he
               attacked her. I tried to defend her but he said -

ACTOR 1 steps forward from wherever he is, fun of fury and aggression.

ACTOR 1   'You are my first son. You should always be on
               my side.'

SAMUEL   And so I got beaten up like my sister. I went to
               college the next day and told my teacher. The
               police got involved.

TAMI   My mum couldn't understand that I was happy
               being gay. She kept saying –

ACTOR 4   'It's a phase.'

TAMI   I said *(provocative again, taunting and leaning into
               ACTOR 4)* 'I've done this' and 'I've done that'…

17

sexual things with men. She was shocked and couldn't believe it. My mother couldn't handle me. It got to the point where she didn't want me to live with her anymore so she put me into children's homes from the age of fourteen.

ALICIA   When I came out at seventeen nobody believed me as I didn't look how they expected a gay person to look or act how they perceive a gay person will act. I moved out of my mum's; me and my mum never got along and I went to live with my step dad and his parents. I was a pretty big drinker by then. I was drinking everyday.

JACK   My parents were abusive because of their own problems. My mother kicked me out of the house. I went and moved in with this girl who I'd only known for two weeks. I was living in her attic and having a strange intense relationship with her which was sexual on her part but on my part I found very difficult to reciprocate but since I'd identified as a dyke, I thought 'ok, we'll go down this road' but that became very abusive. I left her and moved in with my dad who has a terrible drinking problem.

TAMI   I was in four different foster homes. Each one for a year, one was two years. There was one where I was with my sister. She was put into care as well. We could never be split up, we were very close. It was very difficult, living with people you didn't know and they were very strict with you, you couldn't do whatever you wanted, you had to abide by their rules.

ALICIA   I would put my drinking down to having a rocky upbringing as a child and being uncertain about a lot of things including my sexuality. Instead of talking about these things or even thinking about them I'd get wasted instead. I would say I drink because *(steps up from her chair, in a support group now and addressing the room)* I'm an alcoholic and when I drink I can't stop. I've been going to AA for a year. I'm twenty years old. I'll be twenty-one in November.

SAMUEL   The police and social services started to come into my family who at that time started to think that there was something wrong with me. I wasn't 'behaving like an African child' and so that is what prompted my sister to get my phone and see who I was taking to. My sister read my texts and called the number because she thought it was a girl. A guy answered. She asked him if he was gay and he said –

ACTOR 1   *(Perturbed by the random and personal question from the stranger.)* 'Yes'.

SAMUEL   So she told my parents.

ALICIA   I was addicted to Codeine before I started drinking. The Codeine was prescribed to my best friend's grandparents. They got it in huge boxes that were stacked up, enough to last us for months and months. When that ran out my best friend stopped taking it and I started taking my grandparents', I got things from my dad; my step mum was ill and so she was taking Codeine, Tramadol, Diazepam, Temazepam and so I was away with that.

TAMI   One of the foster carers was the worst. The first time I moved in to her house she accused me of stealing and I've never stolen anything in my life, well I did steal things when I was younger. She had another foster child who was about twenty one or twenty two and he said –

ACTOR 3 moves to TAMI and almost whispers the following line to her; quietly threatening.

ACTOR 3   'Turn the TV on or I'll beat the fuck out of you'.

TAMI   That was on my first day there. I was scared for
              my life. He was very manipulative and nasty to
              me. We shared a bedroom and when I'd go to
              bed there were times when his girlfriend was
              there and he'd say –

ACTOR 3   'Turn around and face the wall'

ACTOR 3 firmly manoeuvres TAMI around until she has her back to us.

TAMI   – and I'd hear them having sex.

TAMI; totally humiliated now.

JACK   I stared exploring this feeling that I was trans.
              I went to college with the idea that I would
              finish and transition so I changed my name to
              Alex in an informal way. I'd come out to my
              mum and my brother knew I'd felt like that all
              my life and my best friend from when I was a
              kid had known. Other people who I'd told were
              very, very negative about it and behaved as
              though I didn't know what I was doing or what I
              wanted. I went back in but stuck with the name
              Alex which became a feminine name. People
              were using it with 'she'.

SAMUEL   I was outed. They called a family meeting. I am
              from a very religious family. There were bible
              chapters flying around. I was told they would
              pray for me and help me. We prayed that night
              for a long time. I knew nothing would change. In
              boarding school, there were times when I would
              fast and pray but nothing was changing and you
              know how the Catholics have holy water? Well
              we have an equivalent, Water of Life and the
              water is apparently very powerful. I would bathe
              in that water *(SAMUEL drops to the floor, desperately
              addressing the skies now)* asking to be washed,
              taking the homosexual side out of me.

God knew how much I wanted to ch
He would have changed me if he wante
so I accepted myself in Nigeria for who I wa
There is a picture of me in my mum's bible.

JACK   I went away on my third year to Belgium and
basically had a breakdown and when I came
back I was like, 'things are going to be different
now'. I was trying to get on but there was this
feeling about having to make a change and I
was having these little breakdowns and they
were getting closer and closer together and more
intense and I thought, I've got to do this. It was
do or die basically.

SAMUEL   The next morning we woke up early to pray
(SAMUEL on his knees, praying.) and there was
conversation about sending me back to Africa.
They asked a friend to do something on their
behalf, a person who could take me there and
do it, cure me. It wouldn't be worth it *(SAMUEL
gets up now and moves away, angry and frustrated
at his situation.)* going to Africa, being forced to
change, being humiliated.

JACK   I went back to university and told everyone
what I was doing and that if they didn't like it
they could stick it.

ALICIA   I was drinking every single day. I was taken to
A&E and told that if I stopped drinking I was at
the risk of having a fit. I went back to my mum's
for a fortnight. I stopped drinking cold turkey.
I had a fortnight of hallucinations. *(ALICIA starts
to 'trip', looking around herself in fear and wonder.)*
I tipped my bed to the side so that the bars were
coming through like this *(demonstrates and does so
for the rest of the hallucination she is describing)* and
had the blinds completely closed because things
were coming through the window.

I was seeing things around the bed, under
the sheets. I was hearing stuff and having
conversations with people; people I hadn't
spoken to in years. I was talking as myself and
as a child. I had headaches, nausea; the dealing
with what you'd done when you were drunk.
(ALICIA crawling across the floor now, rock bottom.)
I was constantly tired but unable to sleep. I had
to have all my money, bank cards and ID taken
away from me because as soon as I had them I'd
be out the door to try and buy more alcohol.

TAMI   One of the foster carers would always check if
I was clean after a wash and if she thought I
wasn't she would take me into the bathroom
*(TAMI demonstrates on an imaginary version of
herself, almost as if she has become the Foster Carer;
dragging someone – TAMI – into the bathroom by
the hair.)* hold me down and wash me clean
*(TAMI demonstrates, scrubbing someone in the bath;
aggressive, brutal and dehumanising; humiliating
for the recipient.)* I was seventeen years old at
this point.

ALICIA   I remember bits and bobs and I remember
incidents. It's putting it in the right order that I
struggle with. I know that I have forgotten a lot
when other people recount bits to me later. After
the fortnight the bed was still turned up. I asked
my mother why and she said –

ACTOR 2   'You did that. I don't know why, but you did that'.

SAMUEL   When I was outed my mum cried. The family
felt united. They felt they had found the solution
to all the problems we had. They believed I
behaved in the way I did because I was gay.
My dad would ask me every two weeks if I had
changed. I'd get really angry. There was a series
of incidents in the house. They tried to change

my clothes too because apparently my wardrobe 'made me gay' as well; similar things to what I am wearing now; *(SAMUEL indicates his clothes.)* skinny jeans! My dad didn't want me to go anywhere. He knew I was gay and so he wanted to keep me in, to save me.

TAMI   There were times she would starve me. To this day, the way she was towards me, mentally fucked me up, screwed me up. If I told my social worker it would have got back to my foster parent and I'd be too scared to go home, back to the house.

ALICIA   For me when I was in that situation the only person who could help me was myself but I didn't want to. My family were desperately trying to help me and there wasn't a lot that they could do. I didn't give a shit. *(ALICIA pounds her fist into the wall and then slowly turns back to us, slumped against the wall now, expired.)* It wasn't pleasant for my family. I've got a younger brother who is thirteen now. My brother would have been eleven and I remember one time I had started drinking at an early hour in the morning and he saw me go to the bathroom and I was stumbling *(ALICIA staggers forward.)* and falling against the walls and it scared him so much that he started to throw up.

TAMI   The police came to my flat in 2012. They were doing an investigation regarding one of my foster carers being a child molester, they were investigating sexual abuse. They asked me questions like –

ACTOR 4   'Were you ever sexually touched by any of them you lived with? Were you groped?'

TAMI   I said no. I was shocked. I said, 'can you tell me which one of the foster carers?' and they said –

ACTOR 4   'Sorry we can't.'

TAMI   – but it was obviously someone I lived with.
           I've got no idea who it was.

ALICIA   I wasn't working. I had no responsibilities or
           commitments but my brother was getting up
           at seven in the morning, throwing up and then
           having to go to school. That was a lot of the
           reason why my mum didn't want me in the
           house as she knew what was happening to my
           brother as an effect of my behaviour.

JACK   I started working at Marks and Spencer's and on
           the first day I was working there I came out and
           said *(Addressing the staff room and proudly stating.)*
           'I'm transitioning. I want you to introduce me
           to your staff as "he"'. I was still Alex at the
           time which I changed by deed poll, to get my
           hormones as you need that letter. That name
           wasn't sitting well with me though as it was
           still associated with a female time; a time of
           confusion and so on my last birthday I changed
           it to Jack and I've been taking T for two years
           and I started having surgery in October last year.

TAMI   I was diagnosed with ADD. I was very
           disruptive in class. I had to go to a sort of like
           special school because my behaviour at that time
           was out of control. I got kicked out of school. I
           was sixteen. I didn't do any exams. I don't have
           any GCSEs.

SAMUEL   I went to the police one day about my dad.
           He knew that he couldn't abuse us physically but
           he was abusing us verbally which was worse. He
           was saying a lot that day. I went crazy and told
           the police I was being abused but they couldn't
           do anything as I wasn't being abused physically.

JACK   My relationship with my dad was very difficult;
            he was drinking a ridiculous amount, he always
            has but it was particularly bad at that point.
            He was taking medicine off the internet, just
            random shit that he'd bought and he was being
            particularly unpleasant. He said –

ACTOR 3   'You'd have more friends if you weren't such a
            half-baked bloke'.

JACK   That was hard to take.

SAMUEL   My dad worked at night and so what he'd do
            was sit in the house all morning and talk on the
            phone to people about me. My dad is African.
            Have you heard Africans on the phone on the
            bus? I could hear everything; about how useless
            I am. I would put my earphones in to block to
            the noise. *(SAMUEL sits on the floor and puts his
            headphones in.)* I was surrounded by so much
            negativity. I tried to escape home as much as I
            could, just so that I didn't have to hear anything.

*SAMUEL remains sitting on the floor, pulling his legs in close, trying to
take up as little space as possible. He just wants it all to stop.*

ALICIA   After the cold turkey for two weeks I went to
            Sainsbury's and bought more alcohol. I got
            so drunk that I don't remember anything but
            I was found by some strangers who rang an
            ambulance and I was taken to hospital. I have
            no idea where I was found. That happened quite
            a lot over that period. After the hospital I went
            back to my mums. I got a taxi I think. She was
            like –

ACTOR 2   'You can't stay here anymore. I don't know what
            to do about what you're doing'.

ALICIA   I went back to my Nana's. I ended up living
            there for about a year and a half and at first the
            drinking subsided quite a considerable amount
            and then it crept back up again.

SAMUEL   I would look up singers on Wikipedia to see
         if they were gay friendly and I would listen
         to them and at that time Lady Gaga had just
         come out and I was a massive Lady Gaga fan
         and that hasn't changed and I would listen to
         music to block the voices. I remember her MTV
         acceptance speech when Lady Gaga said –

ACTOR 4   *(With Gaga's New York drawl.)* 'Thanks to the gays.'

ACTOR 4, as Lady Gaga, blows gracious kisses to her adoring gay fans.

SAMUEL   And I was just like 'woooah'. *(SAMUEL jumps into
         the air, elated and suddenly high on life.)* That made
         me want to come out more but I couldn't do it.
         (SAMUEL, less elated now but still hopeful.) I was
         glad someone did it for me.

JACK   I didn't think it was going to fly, like being a
         gay trans man, 'are you taking the piss?' I just
         thought, that's how I feel, I'm attracted to men
         and I feel male so if that's what that is…if that's
         the label for that…then fuck everybody, that's
         what I've got to do and that's basically it. It was
         when I came out as trans that I felt able to come
         out that way as well. It just made so much sense.
         I wasn't going to hide anything anymore.

TAMI   After the four foster homes, I moved into a
         housing association. I was there for about five
         years. That was ok. I had my own bedroom and
         I had to share the kitchen. There was an age
         restriction there, eighteen to twenty three, so
         I had to move out into my own apartment but
         I couldn't handle living on my own. I was in a
         work programme and you have to be there every
         day, Monday to Friday and there were times
         when I wasn't, when I missed appointments.
         They stopped my Job Seekers Allowance for six
         months so I had no money for six months.

My housing benefit was stopped. My rent arrears were going up.

JACK   The crossover in sexuality was funny because all that time I was a lesbian I was collecting pictures of beautiful men but not actually telling anyone about it!

ALICIA   I met somebody on a night out in Newcastle, Emily, who is now my current partner. And I had a job; I worked in a bar, which made me think I could stay behind after work and have a few drinks. But I can't. I can't have 'a few drinks', and I'd buy a bottle on the way home and call in sick to shifts and not go to college and steal alcohol from the house again. One night I was drunk and my Nana came downstairs as I'd woken her up, it was two in the morning and we had a huge argument on the doorstep and my step dad was living there as well and he said –

ACTOR 1   'Don't let her back. She's stealing, she's drinking, you're being too lenient with her. Just don't let her back' –

ALICIA   – and that's what happened.

TAMI   I didn't have any electricity. There was no hot water. I had cold baths. The flat was cold. I didn't have bedding. I didn't have a bed. I had no food.

TAMI; cold and hungry looks around her at her deserted flat. She is alone and helpless.

JACK   Everybody knew about the trans thing but just didn't want to face it. My mother was awful and decided that I'd done it just to upset her. She still calls me Jennifer when she gets excited. Or she'll tell me I'm a good girl and it's just so far away from where I am. I actually found transitioning really easy. I was suddenly interested in people and doing things and in life in general and really excited by everything. I felt really really happy and really enthusiastic about everything.

ALICIA   I went between work, staying at my friends, staying at Emilys and drinking the entire time. When I was seventeen, my step mum died and my dad ran away and disappeared for three months. I went to the flat that he'd abandoned; he'd left the doors unlocked and I just sort of slept over there quite often too.

ALICIA settles herself down for a nights sleep in her father's empty flat.

SAMUEL   I'd get up early in the morning and go to college early even though it started two hours later. After college finished, I would stay on buses. *(SAMUEL sat on the bus now, at a window seat, looking out at the world and the freedom that surrounds him.)* I had a free Oyster card at the time and that just made dad think 'he is going god knows where and doing god knows what'. I would take a long trip from Ilford to Oxford Circus *(SAMUEL looks out the bus window as suburbia turns into the city)* on the Number 25. I'd go to Soho but not know what to do. I didn't get it. I'd go to Oxford Circus and Top Man instead. I had no friends here. Just saying that makes me sound like a Saddo!

ALICIA   I'd be drunk at Emily's. Emily lived with her mum and brother and sister and I got asked to not return. There was a period of time where Emily went on holiday for a weekend and I had nowhere to stay and I rang one of the local Services and asked for emergency housing and because I was over eighteen, I wasn't at risk so those nights I was told –

ACTOR 1   'Just stick it out and if you feel like you're in
            danger you can go to the police station and they
            can turn you out for a few hours'.

ACTOR 1 gives us an insincere smile as he moves onto his next case.

TAMI   I had sex with different men for money. I rented
            myself. It wasn't good. Everyone in Bradford
            knew I was a rent boy. *(ACTORS 1,3 and 4 all turn
            to look at TAMI. They take her in.)* It was the only
            thing I could do. It was the only option. *(Spitting
            out her words now, hurt and ashamed yet defiant too.)*
            I was fighting for my life, trying to stay alive,
            surviving.

JACK   It wasn't comfortable to be at my Dad's. I was
            going from crisis to crisis trying to get by. There
            was no way I could figure out who I was. I was
            going from up to down. I'd quit taking a lot of
            drugs. I'd quit drinking. I'd quit smoking. I was
            trying to get on but he was drinking and being
            abusive and unpleasant and I never knew what
            he was going to be like.

TAMI   I abandoned my flat in Bradford and came
            to Manchester. I met people who became my
            very good friends who are still my very good
            friends now. I stayed in some hostels; Salvation
            Army ones. I was there for a year. I spent my
            Christmas there.

SAMUEL   I wanted to be out the house. I decided to leave.
            Only my sister knew I was leaving. She was the
            one I came out to in Nigeria. My family knew
            I was close to her; we'd gone to Gay Pride
            together in London.

JACK   The Albert Kennedy Trust took me in from
            being at my dad's place which had become
            completely unbearable.

SAMUEL   I didn't even know about Pride. I looked it up.
              I was very excited. *(SAMUEL in the West End now,
              taking in the sights of his first Pride, like a child in
              a candy store, finally fitting in in his own city.)* It
              was so good to go. We went to Oxford Street.
              The whole place was gay, gayed out, many
              organisations supporting different causes, the
              African ones too! It was amazing. My tutor from
              college was also there with her kid. *(Sudden
              shock and realisation.)* She is a lesbian! I was
              wearing a white vest, blue trousers and pink
              shoes and a pink belt. I was very, very, very
              skinny. The pictures of me look horrendous.
              No wonder I got no numbers. I've had a Gok
              Wan Intervention since. We took pictures in
              front of the family house *(The camera flashes as
              SAMUEL poses for a series of ever outlandish selfies, he
              can even pose with one other cast member.)* and put
              the pictures on Facebook. Our siblings are on
              our Facebook and I knew they would tell our
              parents but I didn't care. That's how many fucks
              I didn't give. I didn't care anymore.

ALICIA   I think in my head when I started to sober up
              that is when I got the full fear of what was going
              on. When I had been drinking I just thought, 'I
              can wander with no shoes on'. *(ALICIA does so,
              moving lucidly through her world, no responsibilities,
              free and in free-fall too.)* 'I can go on for days
              living off the land'. I had this false sense of
              security which went away when I stopped
              drinking which was when I ran out of money.
              My best friend was volunteering at Barnardos
              and she arranged for me to meet up with a lady
              at Barnardos to see what I could do.

SAMUEL   I found a leaflet about a LGBT group in East
              London and I went along and they told me
              about the AKT. They told me to go to the

office on Monday. This was on Thursday but I couldn't take another four days, knowing I was almost getting there. I'm a very impatient person. On the Saturday I woke up, took my bag and left.

SAMUEL heads off.

TAMI steps forward, taking centre stage and grabbing her moment.

TAMI I went to Manchester to fit the final piece of the puzzle. I felt a sense of security in Manchester as there is a big gay community. I wanted to be accepted and to become a decent individual. I met Carmel at the AKT and she got me in with a carer. His name was Ben Brookes and he was very nice. There were times we argued about silly things, because I'd done something I shouldn't of. He showed me the ropes, how to survive, how to sort myself out, where to go, how to meet people. I was with him for a year and half.

SAMUEL I went to a bed and breakfast, one bus stop away from my dad's house. That area was all I knew! I thought I'd get a lot of calls that day, normally they ask where you are but they didn't call me. Saturday, no calls, Sunday, no calls, Monday, no calls. If they'd of called me I would have answered. I found it quite surprising. I think it took about a week before my dad called me. I did answer. *(SAMUEL on his mobile phone now, shouting, arguing with his father.)* WE STARTED ARGUING. I HUNG UP.

SAMUEL, quiet and reflective now.

SAMUEL That was the last time we spoke.

TAMI If I hadn't sought help at that time, I would have killed myself.

A brief moment as this information lands with the other cast members.
We move on...

ALICIA   I was referred onto Services. One responded
very quickly and I was called for an interview.
I was offered a room. The place was filled with
loads of different people and if I were to say I
was gay or have Emily around as my partner
it wouldn't be a very good idea. The support
workers recognised that and took me out of the
big lodging and put me in a smaller one, a four
bedroom house with other girls. I was there for a
week. I locked myself in my bedroom. It was the
first time in a long time without any alcohol and
so I had a seizure, collapsed and couldn't move
my legs.

SAMUEL   I was quite frightened the first night I spent out
of the house on my own. The next morning I
had an interview with a Housing Company. I
was sent to this emergency council house in
Ilford. I went shopping and came back and
there was no fridge. I was fucked. I had to put
everything in the oven *(shoves his shopping into the*
oven) so it wouldn't go off!

SAMUEL slams the oven door shut and stares at it. What now?

ALICIA   I ended up in hospital and the service were like –

ACTOR 3   'We can't keep you'

ALICIA   And so I was told in the hospital bed that
afterwards I'd have nowhere to go and –

ACTOR 3   'Whoever wants to pick up your stuff in plastic
bags can do that or we can just bin them for you'.

ALICIA   I went back to my mum's. Every time I drank I
would end up in hospital. She was like –

ACTOR 2   'After last time with your brother, if you drink I've got to say goodbye because I've got to put him first'.

JACK in his own flat now. He is full of wonder.

JACK   Having my own space was amazing. I felt more independent and I became very successful at college after failing all my other courses. I left college that second year with a triple distinction and an unconditional offer to Newcastle University to do fine art. I didn't need any grades to get in. The AKT helped me find a local flat in the area which is absolutely lovely and I am still there now.

ALICIA   I made a decision for my brother. He is very intelligent and he said to me –

ALICIA moves to face ACTOR 1.

ACTOR 1   'It's been really lovely to have you here. It's starting to feel like you're a real sister again.'

ALICIA reaches out for her brothers face and slowly and tenderly strokes it. She looks into his eyes and then suddenly collapses onto his shoulder, crying and breathless, ALICIA relying on her younger sibling for support. After a moment, she pulls herself together and away from her brother.

ALICIA   I had the impending, 'I want to get myself on my feet, I've got to do it myself or it's not working'. There'd been a referral to the AKT put through from the housing centre because in their interview, I ticked a box, 'are you gay, lesbian or trans?'. I normally wouldn't specify but for some reason I just ticked the box and I often think, 'God that was a lucky decision'. Thank god for the lesbian box! I told them pretty much exactly what had happened and they said –

ACTOR 2   'You can come for an interview'.

SAMUEL   I was given money to buy bedding, to buy food. Somehow I survived.

ALICIA   My first interview with Mandy was in April last year and I sort of said what all the problems were and she was like –

ACTOR 2   'We know you go to AA so if you want to tell us when you're going we can make sure you go if that's what you need'.

ALICIA   In May I moved into one of their flats. It was weird having someone offer to help me. It hadn't happened like that before. There was financial help, help if I wanted to work or volunteer or do things in my spare time, help with coming to terms with sexuality, if I needed a referral to another service; like Mental Health or help with keeping doctors' appointments even, everything, a very broad range of things. It was incredible. It takes readjusting to. If feels like you've got lucky and you don't know whether you deserve it. Just little things, somebody asking –

ACTOR 2   'How are you?'

ALICIA   And then from there adjusting to be able to do things I never thought I'd be able to do; like paying a bill.

SAMUEL   Social services went and spoke to my dad. He said it was fine for me to come back and live in the house. I had a white social worker woman. I related more with a woman. I feel more comfortable. Then I got an old Asian guy. I thought 'why have I got an old Asian guy'? I have a bias with black and Asian people. I think they are all going to be homophobic but he was very good, a very nice man.

I was told it was safe for me to go back home and the social services would be coming to check how I am. I spoke to my sister and she said –

ACTOR 2   'No way. He hasn't changed at all.'

SAMUEL   I don't think they will ever change.

ALICIA   What I'd learnt sofa surfing was that I am not safe being openly gay. My sexuality and gender has always made me feel hugely uncomfortable.

TAMI   I started to transition. I started dressing up as a girl. I ended one chapter and created a new one. I didn't see a psychiatrist. I started self-medicating, buying hormones from the internet. My breasts started to grow, my hair was long. My hair changed. It grew quicker. What I am taking now, it changes the hair pattern, the shape of the hair.

JACK   We went to see my auntie *(JACK now at his auntie's home, physically he should be separate from the other cast at this point, isolated.)* and I'd just had surgery and I was sitting there with stitches in my chest; I hadn't been home, we'd just gone straight there, I'd just come out the theatre a couple of hours earlier and I'm sitting there and they were talking about me in the room and saying –

ACTOR 2   'She this…' –

JACK   – and –

ACTOR 4   'She that…' –

JACK   – and using my birth name –

ACTORS 2, 3 and 4 all take a moment to repeatedly say and whisper the name 'Jennifer', the name ripples around the room, bouncing off each wall.

JACK – and I remember, I hadn't thought it until now, and I just remember feeling so upset and invisible and thinking 'do you fucking realise I've just gone and had a double mastectomy and I'm sitting here in this pain and you're blatantly trashing who I am and what I've just done to support that'. My Auntie said it was disgusting and proceeded to call me Jennifer and my mother joined in as she thought it was more important to preserve my Auntie's feelings than mine.

TAMI Living as a woman was great, fantastic. I couldn't tell my mum. She is very private. I am very direct. I don't hide anything from anyone, even though I should. I couldn't have told my mother because of the reaction I got when I told her I was gay. I couldn't tell her I was becoming a girl! When I told her it took her two years to accept it. I didn't speak to my mum for two years. I'm still self-medicating. There can be side effects, blood clots, strokes, heart attacks, liver failure. My doctor's advising me not to take them but I can't wait. I take pills every day.

JACK It's more wounding when it comes from somewhere close like that, not when someone shouts something when you're walking down the street. I see my dad a lot more these days as he's really grown as a person and I ring him every other day and try and tell him what's going on and *(resigned to the fact she's his Mum after all)* I love my mum anyway.

SAMUEL I applied to study law. I was told by my teachers to apply to Oxford but I didn't want to because my dad wanted me to! I applied to the London School of Economics. I went to the interview *(SAMUEL bounces into the interview room.)* and it turned into this gay thing.

ACTOR 4   'Tell me a time when you overcame a particular issue?'

SAMUEL   'I was gay and homeless blah blah blah'.

SAMUEL horrified at himself again, realising he just can't stop himself.

ACTOR 4   'And a time when you had to think outside the box?'

SAMUEL regains his confidence.

SAMUEL   'Because I am gay blah blah blah'. *(SAMUEL horrified again but laughing at himself too.)* I don't think it went well but I got a place. I want to go into law; family law.

ALICIA   I was in that flat for almost a year. I was sad to leave it. *(ALICIA looks fondly around the empty room.)* Once I'd cleaned out all my stuff and it looked the same as when I first moved in. It felt very nostalgic. That was the very first home that I'd built. With moving out before, it's always been on a whim or not exactly by choice. It was the first time leaving a place and only having good memories of it which I'd not had before.

ALICIA takes in the room around her for a moment and then suddenly perks up as her location transfers to her new flat now.

ALICIA   I moved three weeks ago with the AKT on a tenancy agreement. I love my new flat. Just got my wifi, really happy, totally love it!

TAMI   I still see the person I was born as. When someone says, 'that's a man', I get really pissed off and it really affects my confidence. My transition is a struggle. In my opinion transsexuality is not heard enough. People fear us because we are different and born in the wrong body, trying to change our body to the body we are meant to be in.

JACK   People are frightened about what to say as they don't want to offend. If someone is generally interested and wants to understand then I am more than happy to answer any questions.
        If we want people to understand us we have to be willing to tell people things. I want to try and share some of the experiences of trans people.

SAMUEL My first experience with trans people, I said *(SAMUEL points out, in total shock, not intentionally mean.)* 'she's a tranny', everyone was shocked –

The cast surround SAMUEL, not ganging up on him though.

SAMUEL – I was told –

ACTOR 4 'No, you don't say that'.

SAMUEL I had no idea. I'm happy now that I've learnt this.

JACK   People may be threatened by their own sexuality and they don't want to look at themselves, how it may apply to them. They may think it's about sex, as an activity, but it's got nothing to do with that.

TAMI   I want people to realise that I have a huge history in my life and I have so many goals. I'm fighting. Surviving to get to where I need to. I think everyone's life is a constant battle. Everyone is trying to get to the top

JACK   I had to learn how to carry myself, to behave. It's something you pick up socially, subconsciously and I wasn't taught that. I don't have that history. It's something I am still learning. I'm having to go into the men's toilets like *(JACK swaggers into the Gents.)* 'I fucking own this place!' You can't go scurrying in! I'm still learning about gay male culture, in terms of how it works, the interactions between people and what they mean.
        It's completely new to me.

TAMI   I don't have boyfriends. I have dates with
        straight men. They know because on the
        websites I put down that I am a trans woman
        and so they are either into that or not. I don't
        have a problem disclosing. If someone asks me
        if I am a man or woman, I won't lie.

JACK   I've had instances where someone has found me
        attractive and they found out later I was trans,
        or they found me attractive before I transitioned
        and then they can't speak to me anymore.
        I tread that line in the middle. It does make
        people uneasy. Their identity is threatened by
        mine and sometimes that's great because I've
        helped people come out and then other times it's
        made things very difficult.

SAMUEL In some aspects you can always read me but
        when it comes to dating I am very hard to read.
        I have had a lot of problems with dating. People
        who like me, I don't like. People I like, don't like
        me. I think, 'ok, I'm a good looking guy, any
        guy should want to be with me!'

TAMI   There are certain times when I do want to be in
        a relationship with a man but it's very difficult
        for them if they've never been in a relationship
        with a transsexual woman before. They can never
        hold my hand in public, never kiss me in public,
        never show affection because they are worried
        about how people would think about them.

JACK   If I meet somebody who understands me
        generally, I don't think it will be an issue.
        If it goes wrong, it goes wrong. It's just
        something I have to try and see what happens.

SAMUEL If I was with a white guy my parents would think
        it reinforced the belief that being with a white
        person has made this person gay. My parents
        think being gay is a 'white thing'.

> They think it's something unfortunate that irresponsible white men do that some black people have unfortunately picked up. We have to change that.

JACK   I want to go to this bar called the Eagle where they don't let women downstairs. I was out the other week for somebody's birthday and there was this really nice guy there called Paul and he's a personal trainer and he was all big and he couldn't leave me alone, he was like –

ACTOR 3 slaps his hand down on JACK's knee and gives it a squeeze.

ACTOR 3   'I love little guys.'

JACK   And he didn't know! I've been with a guy since November who already knew. He was my manager at Marks and Spencer's.

JACK gives us a confident and cheeky smile; 'I've pulled'.

ALICIA   When I was living in places before, I didn't want to be there. I wanted to be elsewhere. I couldn't cope with the people. I couldn't cope with myself so I would drink. I started to learn more and more about my own drinking. Clearly I was depressed when I was drinking and when you're depressed you don't care about anything.

TAMI   I've written a book. You'll like it. It's from my own word of mouth. It'll explain even more about me and what I've gone through. For me, writing my story down, I felt a sense of freedom. When I write, I feel like I'm walking in the sand at the beach. I can feel the wind and the breeze. If you asked me to write a poem now I would write it. At home I've got a folder of poems. They are all about personal experiences. It won't take me long to write a poem.

JACK   Where I work it's really rough. People there
don't know anything about this kind of thing
and there is this lady, hard as nails, and she rang
me up the other night and said –

JACK and ACTOR 4 on the phone now.

ACTOR 4   'When you joined the shop I didn't know what
you were about and I didn't want to know but
I have seen you change so much and I am so
proud of you and what you have been through.
I can't tell you how much I admire you and
don't let anybody hold you back or bring you
down and if you ever need anything I am here
for you… son.'

*ACTOR 4 and then JACK, who is astounded, maybe they both are, both
hang up.*

JACK   You'd think she'd be prejudiced but being
around me and seeing who I am as a person
she was able to get me, somebody I didn't think
would and she didn't think she would. I felt like
I had somehow been able to open her mind.
We are not even that close.

*TAMI steps into the light, ready to recite her poem, about to emotionally
open herself up before us; brittle but brave too.*

TAMI   My outside doesn't match my insides yet.

             Sometimes

             it feels as though

             I am carrying many

             bodies in me

             more than one life

             lots of beginnings, former selves

             many possible ends.

It's a long journey back to yourself

Unlearning

the kind of loneliness that withers you.

learning a smile with no grief in it.

You fall you get up you fall down again

get pushed,

get it punched out of you.

Get scared,

get strong again.

Get up

It takes a whole lot of strength trying to be who you are.

what you are meant for

what you might have been

what you will be.

what you've always been

what you almost are

Out here doesn't match what's in there yet

still

things will only ever get better

I see who I am becoming

blossoming in the quiet.

Claiming me as my own creation

grasping who I am, tight.

JACK   Hormonally I am fifteen or sixteen. I do feel that way. I do feel that young. I've got a life which has made me experience so much. I feel old but there is this other part of me which is very naive and vulnerable. When I was growing up the first time, I stopped, I was frozen in time. I never became a woman. I didn't get past fourteen, fifteen years of age. I'm trying to make that up now.

ALICIA   When you're a teenager you tend to form your identity and I didn't do that as I was always out of my head and drinking was my identity. When I sobered up it was like I was going back to being thirteen and so I had to learn about responsibility and who I am and all that other beautiful soul searchy stuff. When I was drinking I didn't have hobbies or interests or a personality but now that I'm not drinking there are things I'm interested in that I just wasn't before. I take it a day at a time. If I look too far ahead I get a bit 'wooo'.

JACK, SAMUEL, ALICIA and TAMI back on their seats now, in the interview room as we first met them.

JACK   I thought about not doing this. Is it worth doing? Have I got anything to say? And I thought, 'I have' and also it's flattering that someone would want to use my story. I was asked and I thought that it might help my whole journey. I hope I do a good job of representing trans people.

TAMI   I'm looking forward to someone else telling my story through their eyes.

SAMUEL   I did think something like this would happen. Maybe I just want to be an actor or a star. I'm hopeful that one day I'll be acting in this. I want to play myself. Why would anyone else be playing me? I could do that!

ALICIA   I never thought I'd be interviewed. Unless it was in court!

TAMI   I don't know what the reaction will be; if it's a good one or bad one. That's really difficult to answer. This is overwhelming.

ALICIA   I like the idea of there being a big giant LGBT community where we can share our stories. I like hearing what other people have to say. Historically people that are LGBT have been quietened and I think the more we actually hear from them and not other people speaking on their behalf, the more we're going to learn. I think that it's constantly moving forward in little dribs and drabs and the only way to keep it going is with some serious traction.

SAMUEL   People strangely say they find my story moving or touching. I don't want people to have certain feelings about my story. There is no intent on my side to make them feel a certain way as long as they are not thinking 'get this attention seeker out of my face!'

JACK   I want people to know I am just a person. They are no different from me. I don't want them to feel intimidated or threatened by what they may perceive as my difference. I don't feel that different. This is what's normal for me. I have to remind myself what it's like for other people. Sometimes I think that people don't know how to respond and so draw away. I hope that people who see this will have an understanding, a connection.

SAMUEL   Family means… I don't know if it means anything. It means the people you surround yourself with. It could be your handmade family, it could be your biological family… if they want you.

JACK   It means people you can feel safe around.

TAMI   To me family means everything.

ALICIA   It means 'home'. It means feeling comfortable.
              It means feeling that you can be yourself and
              not be judged. It doesn't feel fearful or scary.

SAMUEL   Life isn't simple for everyone. Some people
              are lucky to have parents that are cool. It's not
              as easy as everyone thinks. You always need
              communities. Even if society got to the point
              where everyone is ok with everyone, we still
              need communities.

TAMI   What I would say to my younger self would be
              to choose the right path for yourself because no
              one else can chose it for you.

SAMUEL   I would say to not worry too much, to know that
              things always sort themselves out.

ALICIA   I'd tell her to keep on trucking on.

JACK   I would say put yourself first. If I had kids
              I would teach them that what they thought
              counted. I would teach them how to form
              opinions.

TAMI   I would teach them right from wrong, to be
              polite, to be honest, to be open minded and not
              to judge or discriminate.

ALICIA   I'd teach them to be open and understanding
              and to listen, to be able to stand back from a
              situation before jumping in, to be able to form
              an opinion and have morals.

SAMUEL   I'd teach them to eat healthily, no junk food.
              I feel safe when I know the future. I'm not
              spontaneous as a person. Living at my parents',
              hearing my father say things, my heartbeat
              would be racing.

JACK steps forward and heads downstage, to one side of the stage.

JACK   I feel safe when I am in the back of the car,
       looking out of the window. I can just relax.

TAMI steps forward and joins JACK downstage.

TAMI   I don't think anyone's ever safe in their life.
       We may have perfect homes with alarms but
       we're not safe. I could get hit by a bus tomorrow.
       We're never safe.

JACK   I feel unsafe at work. I have anxiety attacks,
       panics and issues with sleeping as it feels so
       unsafe.

TAMI   I feel least safe when I'm surrounded by strangers.

SAMUEL gets up and joins TAMI and JACK, all three of them lined up downstage.

SAMUEL I felt least safe living at my parents. Definitely.
       Safe means security, knowing your future.
       Feeling settled. Having peace of mind.
       Having nothing to worry about.

JACK   Safe is something solid like when someone
       heavy lays on me and I feel totally squashed.
       That feels safe.

ALICIA joins JACK, TAMI and SAMUEL downstage now, all four of them lined up and facing out.

ALICIA   Like now, even. Just little things, like you unlock
       the door when you go in and put the heating on
       and you know that you've got food.

TAMI   What does 'safe' mean to me? Closure.
       Once my life is closed into a little box and it's
       got a lock on it and no one can get into it.
       I'm not there yet. No. That's not the best way to
       explain it. I've got it; what 'safe' means to me.

I'll give you four different words. Security, acceptance, freedom and *(Long pause.)* ... I need a word for E...security, acceptance, freedom and...equality. That's what 'safe' means to me.

TAMI, JACK, ALICIA and SAMUEL look out at us as the lights dim and footage of a city street at night, with the accompanying soundtrack of sirens, passing traffic and chattering voices, is projected onto them. They continue to look out at us as the cityscape dances across their faces and bodies until, after a moment, the footage suddenly stops and we are all plunged into complete darkness.

END

WWW.OBERONBOOKS.COM